P9-CDY-202

LITTLE
HIDDEN
PICTURES

Tony and Tony
Tallarico

DOVER PUBLICATIONS, INC.
Mineola, New York

Copyright

Copyright © 2008 by Tony and Tony Tallarico
All rights reserved.

Bibliographical Note

Little Hidden Pictures is a new work, first published by
Dover Publications, Inc., in 2008.

International Standard Book Number

ISBN-13: 978-0-486-46581-4
ISBN-10: 0-486-46581-0

Manufactured in the United States by Courier Corporation
46581003
www.doverpublications.com

Note

Get ready to look for pumpkins, candy canes, umbrellas, and baseballs and many other objects hidden in the twenty-four picture puzzles in this fun-filled book. Each puzzle has a box at the bottom that shows you pictures of the objects to look for, as well as exactly how many of each one you will find. Color in each object as you find it—and count up the number of items when you're done. There's even a Solutions section after the puzzles, in case you need to check your answers. When you're done, you can color in all of the pages. Have fun!

Find: 7 - 🌼🌼🌼🌼🌼🌼🌼

4 - 🏈🏈🏈🏈 1 - 🎃

1 - 🍎

Football and pumpkins and leaves
to be raked—it must be fall.

4

Look carefully for the 18 objects
hidden in this autumn picture.

5

Find: 5- 😊 😊 😊 😊 😊

3- ☆ ☆ ☆   3- 🐟 🐟 🐟

1- 🐕 🧢 🐢 ⛺ 🖌️

Here's a funny picture—
a circus in the snow!

6

There are 16 objects hidden in the
scene—can you find them all?

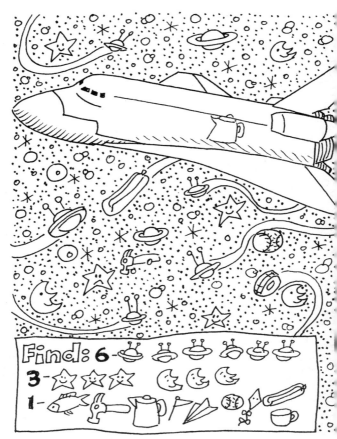

Space exploration helps us
learn about our universe.

Find 21 objects hidden in this picture.

These friends are having quite an
adventure in their rowboat.

Find 5 fish and 13 other objects
hidden in the picture.

Find: 3 - 🍬🍬🍬 2 - 🐰🐰

2 - 🌿🌿 1 - 🍎 🐕 ⛸

1 - 🏒 🦴 📓 🌵 ☆ 🌙 🔨 📦

Everyone's enjoying outdoor
sports in this winter scene.

12

Look carefully through the snowflakes
to find 18 hidden objects.

Maybe this soccer player will kick
the ball into the goal!

While we're waiting for the kick, find 21 objects hidden in this busy picture.

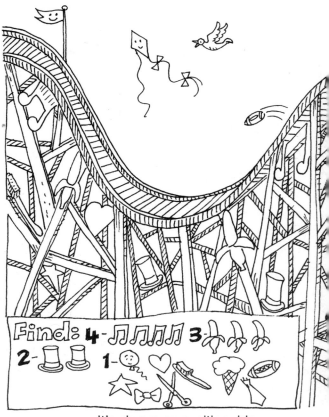

It's always an exciting ride
on a roller coaster!

Believe it or not, there are 18 objects
for you to find in this scene.

Some people enjoy growing their
own vegetables in a garden.

18

Look for 5 flowers and 14 other
objects in this outdoor picture.

There's a lot happening in this
picture of a rider and a cowboy.

Can you find all 19 objects in this
picture—including 6 horseshoes?

Here are a couple of ways to
spend a fine summer day.

Now look at the picture and find 19
objects hidden in the backyard.

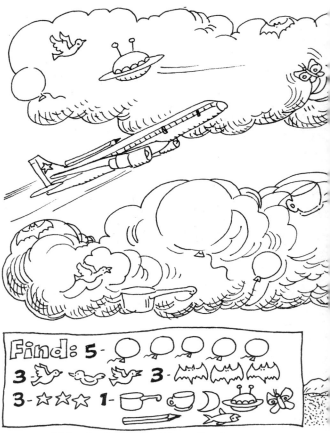

Find: 5 - 🎈🎈🎈🎈🎈
3 - 🕊🐦🕊   3 - 🦇🦇🦇
3 - ☆☆☆   1 - 🍵 ✏️ ☕ 🌙 🛸 🦋 🐟

This sky is filled with puffy clouds
and many other objects.

24

Find 5 balloons floating in the air,
and 16 other things, too.

25

Find: 5 🌼🌼🌼🌼🌼
4- 🎵🎵🎵🎵 2- ☂☂
1- 🪚 🍊 ⚓ 🍌 🧦 〜 ❤

These travelers are lucky to see so
many animals on their safari.

Look carefully at this picture and
find 18 hidden objects.

Find: 5 — 🍎 🍎 🍎 🍎 🍎
4 —
3 — 1 — ♡

The Princess greets the Prince in
this storybook scene.

Hidden in this pleasant picture
are 19 objects—find them all.

Find: **2**

1

The Queen is having
her portrait painted.

30

Find 2 birds and 13 objects in
the scene at the castle.

Find: 5- 🍦🍦🍦🍦🍦
3- 🍄🍄🍄   2- 🪴🪴🪴
1- 📘 🥕 ✉ 🐟 〰 🎆

Everyone is running to get ice cream.
Summer must be here!

In addition to 5 ice-cream cones, find
12 other objects in the picture.

Ellen is about to give her answer
in this math classroom.

Look carefully at the picture and
find 18 hidden objects.

Find: 8 -
6 -
1 -

Here's a scene showing some
dinosaurs that lived long ago.

There are 21 objects hidden in this picture—
look carefully and find them all.

Splashing in the water
is great fun!

Find 2 balloons and 15 other hidden
objects in this playful picture.

Find: 5 - ☆☆☆☆☆
4 - 🧢🧢🧢
2 - ⚾⚾ 🌸 🦉🦉
1 - 🛷 🪥 ❤️ 🐟 🧹

It's time for this family to relax after a
busy week of work and school.

Find 4 baseball caps and 17 other
hidden objects in this picture.

There's water, water, everywhere in this
soggy scene!

Jump between the raindrops to find 16
objects hidden in this picture.

Jill and Jeremy are surprised at how many
animals have come to greet them.

There are 16 objects hidden in this picture—
can you find them all?

Find: 5 - [shells] 4 - [crayons] 3 - [sails] 1 - [gift] [fish] [star] [bird]

Everyone has something fun
to do at the beach today!

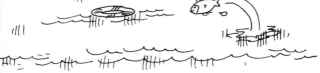

Look from side to side and up and down to
find 20 hidden objects in this scene.

47

It's Halloween, and these friends
are out trick-or-treating.

Find 5 bats, 3 pumpkins, and 13 other
objects hidden in this scary scene.

49

Find: 5 - 🍬🍬🍬🍬🍬
4 - 🎀🎀🎀🎀   3 - 👜👜👜
2 - 😊😊   1 - 🍎

These Christmas trees are beautifully
decorated for the holiday.

Look carefully and find 5 candy canes and
14 other objects hidden in this picture.

SOLUTIONS

pages 4-5

pages 6-7

pages 8-9

pages 10-11

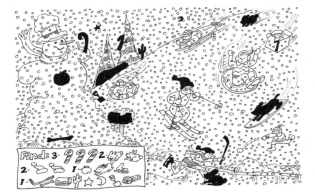

pages 12-13

pages 14-15

55

pages 16-17

pages 18-19

pages 20-21

pages 22-23

pages 24-25

pages 26-27

Find: 5 🍎🍎🍎🍎🍎
4 - 🍂🍂🍂🍂
3 - 🐌🐌🐌 1 - 🌸 🐛 ⭐ 🌾

pages 28-29

Find: 2 - ✂️✂️ 🔪🔪 🏹🏹 🖌️🖌️
1 - ⭐ 🍾 🏹 ❤️ 🚗 💧

pages 30-31

pages 32-33

pages 34-35

pages 36-37

pages 38-39

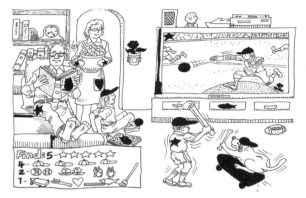

pages 40-41

pages 42-43

pages 44-45

pages 46-47

pages 48-49

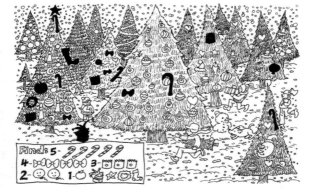

pages 50-51